IOWA

Celebrating the Sesquicentennial

Essays by

Bill Wundram, Tricia DeWall, Jeffrey Bruner, Tom Thoma, and Bill Zahren

AMERICAN & WORLD GEOGRAPHIC PUBLISHING

KENNETH LAYMAN

Right: Oat stacks on an Amish farm near Kalona.
Below: Moving up the Mississippi, near Marquette.
Facing page: The Ashmore-Jewell barn, dating from 1868, near Decorah and Luther College.

Title page: The sun rises on Fish Farm Mounds, Indian burial sites in the northeast corner of the state just past Lansing.
P. MICHAEL WHYE PHOTO

Front cover: Late afternoon farm scene at West Branch.
NORMAN POOLE PHOTO
Back cover: April Johnson has her hands full (of accomplishment).
MORNING STAR PHOTO

STEPHEN GASSMAN

ISBN 1-56037-085-8

© 1995 American & World Geographic Publishing
Text pages 5-13 © 1995 Bill Wundram
Text pages 31-35 © 1995 Tricia DeWall
Text pages 49-54 © 1995 Jeffrey Bruner
Text pages 71-77 © 1995 Tom Thoma
Text pages 93-98 © 1995 Bill Zahren

Write for our catalog:

American & World Geographic Publishing, P.O. Box 5630, Helena, MT 59604, or call 800-654-1105
Printed in U.S.A.

Library of Congress Cataloging-in-Publication Data
Iowa : celebrating the sesquicentennial / with essays by Bill
    Wundram ... [et al.].
       p.   cm.
    ISBN 1-56037-085-8 (pbk.)
    1. Iowa--Description and travel.   2. Iowa--Geography.
3. Iowa--Pictorial works.   I. Wundram, Bill.
F621.I59 1995   95-24360
917.77--dc20

Contents

Above: The Wapsipinicon River near Anamosa.
Right: The Village of East Davenport, once the sight of a large Civil War encampment, is now a favorite shopping area.

Facing page: The essence of rural Iowa, northeast of Kalona.

EASTERN IOWA

by Bill Wundram

While flying cross-country, my New York City seat mate seemed puzzled by my love affair with Iowa. His questioning opened large answers, and I could best reply: "Alabama is the South, and the North is the North, and California is California, but Iowa is America."

Innocently put, that was my answer, and when I muse over Iowa—particularly the eastern tier of the state of which I am particularly fond—I like to repeat the conviction of Donald Kaul, writing in the *Washington Post*:

"Iowa is graced by absolutely marvelous people. I know you hear that all the time, but it's true. They are clean, brave, thrifty, reverent, loyal, honest and able to brush after every meal."

There is no corn-fed dogma or theory of how each Iowa city, or wide-spot-in-the-road or religious sect, can fit into a jigsaw puzzle of fence rows and slick city streets. I have never been able to talk about such things without telling stories of people and places.

Along the eastern borders of Iowa, and stretching inland, it was always the river that was the preeminent reason for the founding and growth of hamlets that grew into big cities, and other hamlets that stayed that way. The big river—the Mississippi—that was it! Why, it even brought Mark Twain to Muscatine, where he worked as a printer's devil, and the only thing he wrote about it, and much remembered, was that the city had beautiful sunsets, and that he was once chased by a man he thought was a lunatic.

Right: Dubuque, Iowa's oldest city, celebrates its special site on the Mississippi River every year with the autumn RiverFest.
Below: A fall frost graces the resting land of Washington County.

Facing page: Why Iowa is America.

We've had our share of lunatics—or people who really weren't, but some thought they were. One of the earliest contenders was Giacomo Constantine Beltrami, a handsome, dark-eyed former officer in the Italian Army on his way to find the true source of the Mississippi River in the year 1823. The only way was by steamboat, and none had ever traveled north of the dreaded Rock Island Rapids opposite what is now Davenport. The Mississippi was a wilderness river, flowing past unpeopled forest, bluff and prairie. But the grubby steamboat he was aboard (the *Virginia*) bounced through the frothy, rock-jagged water. Not, however, until Beltrami had paused to visit with the Sauk Indians camping in the hills. He waltzed and spoke to them in his native Italian tongue. They thought he was a madman. A true con of his time, he convinced the Sauk that he was from the moon, a celestial being, and left for the steamboat

with bundles of furs and beads, which he promised to carry with him upon his return to the promised land in the sky.

It would seem the first settlers in Iowa were not from the staid, respected eastern United States, but adventurous Frenchmen, who left their own marks not only upon Iowa, but all of America. The earliest bona fide settler in Lee County was Louis Honore Tesson, a Frenchman who established the first apple orchard not only in Iowa, but west of the Mississippi River. A stone marks the spot today at 5th and Main streets in Montrose. In 1795, Basil Girard, a Frenchman, received a humongous grant of 5,680 acres in what is now Clayton County from the King of Spain—the first European settler after the Louisiana Purchase. He settled down and promptly married a silken-skinned Indian maiden.

The land-hungry settlers were soon to come, hardy pioneers with ax in hand and rifles on their shoulders, pushing the native Americans aside after the Black Hawk War. They were awed, as visitors are yet today, by the wonders of Iowa's Mississippi River in the lands of Allamakee County, with majestic bluffs and where the river—to this day—drops seven feet a mile. This is the land of McGregor and Guttenburg, where explorers Marquette and Joliet, paddling their Indian canoes down the Wisconsin River, gazed upon the magnificent land and proclaimed it "Little Switzerland."

Soon, the railroad was to come, but how to cross the wide, almost unmanageable, Mississippi River? Once, a locomotive was pushed across the frozen ice, but a bridge was needed. Most engineering minds did not consider it economically feasible. But at Davenport, a bridge *was* built, in 1856—a milestone landmark—of 10-inch-square oak timbers, painted brilliant white and strong enough to support an entire railroad train. Jubilation!

The first bridge across the big river! Whistles blew. Cannons fired. It lasted a mere two weeks. Its draw span burned to embers when struck by a side wheeler, the *Effie Afton*. It was rebuilt, but bitter steamboat interests, envisioning the end of their monopoly on traffic, later absurdly filed charges of murder against the bridge after a fatal steamboat mishap at the draw. Losing that round, they sued, contending that railroads had no right to bridge navigable streams, threatening the safety of river traffic. They lost. The railroads had hired a good attorney—a lanky fellow from Springfield, Illinois, named Abraham Lincoln.

With or without the railroad, the West was opening across the wide Mississippi River, not without boastful claims and quick prosperity and expect-

ed mayhem. In the Big Woods along the Maquoketa River, a desperate band of outlaws looted and plundered. Counterfeiting and horse stealing were their chief aims, with an occasional murder thrown in for good measure. Respectable citizens banded together in a militia and cleaned out the highwaymen in what came to be known as "The Bellevue War."

Cedar Rapids came into being with broadsides of the 1840s making "particular reference to the convenience of the county and the healthfulness of the location." In its first decade, though, a band of outlaws used the present Municipal Island as a rendezvous until the gang was broken up in 1851. By the 1870s, Cedar Rapids was boom town, and in 1886 it popped its buttons when Brucemore was built, hailed by architects as the finest residence this side of Chicago. Its Queen Anne style entertained the greats, the likes of Presidents Hoover and Truman. It is the only property in Iowa endowed by the National Trust for Historic Preservation. Today, I think of Cedar Rapids as a handsome, hustling city, rising suddenly from the prairie off Interstate 380, with its Five Seasons Civic Center, its essence of Quaker Oats to remind visitors of breakfast time, and beautiful Bohemian girls.

Life in the founding days, though, was tough, primitive, lonely. In southeast Iowa, mail was brought in by a carrier who walked the county, tromping down tall prairie buffalo grass and stumbling through timber from Wapello to tiny mud-laned settlements in Washington County. There was only twice-monthly delivery.

Every nook and hollow sought prominence and respectability. Into this new land, counties were carved into the lower sections of the Mississippi River boundaries. Often, they had quirky names. Louisa County was named for Louisa Massey, who acquired wide fame when she shot down a ruffian who had killed one of her brothers and was attempting to murder another.

Above: Still life with moon, near Elkader.

Facing page: Virginia bluebells (Mertensia virginica) *splash Eastern Iowa with color.*

Voila! Eastern Iowa grew. Towns and county seats puffed with pride, but the dilemma of getting from here to there was agonizing. One of the early Eastern Iowa experiments was the Plank Road, an idea borrowed from the eastern states. The scheme was to lay planking, as our concrete pavement is used today. Henry County found the experiment so-so, but the concept was bolstered by James Smyth, a respected judge of the 20th Iowa District who hailed Plank Roads as important civic improvements "to open this grand new State of Iowa to the populace of all." Upon his advice, a wooden road was laboriously built for 22 miles from Burlington to Mount Pleasant. Of course, the Plank Roads were an easily mired fiasco. Yet, today, an occasional road plank is dug by an amused farmer planting corn.

Above: In a state with thousands of miles of rivers and streams, it's easy to stake out a good spot, this one just south of the Quad-Cities.

Facing page: The Quad-City Times Bix 7, held the last weekend in July, draws thousands. It coincides with the Bix Beiderbecke Memorial Jazz Fest, one of the nation's top Dixieland events, inspired by Davenport's own famous cornetist.

Some dream towns turned into nightmares. M.V. Burris platted a town bearing his name at a junction where he thought a new railroad would cross the Mississippi just above the Iowa River. His agents hurried back East to enlist capital, with wonderful maps and colored lithographs showing a thriving metropolis that existed mostly as a figment of imagination. At the first flood, the fledgling town of a handful of houses was submerged. Lives and property were lost and Burris' dream city became a deserted village. Eastern investors were enraged.

Iowa was now the 29th state in the promising new union. Old Capitol, a masterpiece of Greek Revival architecture built in Iowa City, served as Iowa's territorial and then first state capitol from 1852 until 1857, when the capital moved to Des Moines. The original capitol is a hallmark of restoration. With a towering self-supporting reverse spiral staircase, its top step is directly above its bottom step. It seems magically suspended in the air.

Yet, with a grandiose state capitol in Eastern Iowa, and while starch-collared legislators debated inside, the confused settlers on the outside had little help in knowing where they were going. As a guide to their westward journeying, a husky farmer named Lyman Dillon was employed to plow—by oxen—a hundred-mile furrow from what is now Clinton Street in Iowa City to Dubuque. The furrow later extended from Iowa City to Burlington. There is little to claim that it was of much use, after the first cloudburst mushed the furrow.

In this green, untested state, there was money to be made. The railroad had reached Iowa City, and a preacher from Virginia wrote back home: "I gave $10 an acre for a 2,000-acre tract west of Cedar County. I think I got an excellent bargain. People tell me that I can sell it in the spring for $15 an acre." Farmers, buying land at such bargain prices in Eastern Iowa, found the black soil to be rich beneath the head-high prairie grass. In plowing the grass into the soil, many developed an agonizing rash that laid raw their loins. It was a common malady called "Prairie Itch," but it could be cured with a smarting new ointment called Sloan's Liniment.

Using the materials at hand, many communities prospered. At Stone City—made famous by artist Grant Wood—the Anamosa limestone plunged 60 feet into the ground for miles and was dug and picked and blasted at a handsome profit. Its limestone still buttresses hundreds of Iowa buildings. Grant Wood was born at Stone City; his painting of the humped hills and rounded trees, called "Stone City," is nearly as notable as his "American Gothic." His works portray persons and places still easily recognized by citizens of Jones County.

As if on cue, religious groups discovered Iowa. Mormon converts from Europe and eastern American states bundled their kids and belongings and organized in Iowa the exhausting Handcart Expedition, heading to their New Jerusalem in Utah.

Not far from Iowa City, another culture flourishes—Kalona, often called Amish-land, with its hitching posts and clip-clopping buggies. Mennonites, who revert back to the Protestant Reformation in Europe, share the simple beliefs of pacifism. There is no ostentation in dress. Beards for the men and black bonnets for the ladies, and a simple—sometimes diffident—way of life where Old Order members shun electrical power and all popular conveniences.

To the north, lumber-jacketed woodsmen were stripping the forests bare. Pineries of Minnesota and Wisconsin floated vast rafts of logs downstream to the mills of Clinton and Muscatine. Clinton, at the turn of the 20th century, claimed 17 millionaires, all produced by the lumbering industry. A few of their gabled mansions linger in the bluffs. The good old days are still remembered in Clinton. Its Class A baseball team is called the LumberKings.

In the 1850s, the supply of lumber from the northland appeared inexhaustible. The rafters and house siding from Muscatine lumber mills was said to have built the Midwest. Then, suddenly a unique new Muscatine industry developed. J.B. Boepple discovered that the shells of freshwater mussels adapted to pearl buttons.

"Mine buttons will make you rich," the German would shout on the

Above: Morning shower—Bridal Veil Falls in Pikes Peak State Park southeast of McGregor.
Facing page: Burlington's famed Snake Alley, which is often compared to San Francisco's Lombard Street.

streets of Muscatine. They made many people rich. At one time, 4,000 were employed in the button industry. Along came plastic. Well, you know what happened, then, to the pearl button.

Visitors to Iowa follow the life and career of Herbert Hoover, who came home to be buried in West Branch, Iowa, in 1964, the little town he left nearly 80 years before. In a 200-acre tract, tourists are awed by the comparison of his impressive Presidential Library, beside the humble two-room birthplace cottage where red tulips (the favorite flower of the president's mother) blossomed every springtime.

Davenport is energetic, bustling, with 100,000-plus people. Davenport's once famed Gold Coast, blocks of mansions, is now being painstakingly restored. Their wide porches overlook a twist where the Mississippi River inexplicably runs east and west, instead of north and south. Both Davenport and its adjoining friend, Bettendorf, have giant gambling boats, enterprising tourism lures. Davenport's RiverCenter is a mammoth, striking attraction for public events; its Putnam Museum of History and Natural Science is the finest in all of Iowa—only museums in places like Minneapolis, Denver and St. Louis are comparable. Davenport's Municipal Art Museum is the envy of much larger cities.

By building the first bridge across the Mississippi, Davenport claims it opened the American West, and that is likely true when historians measure the significance with the pounding of the golden spike. Its annual Daven-

KENNETH LAYMAN

port Bix Beiderbecke Festival, in honor of its late, lamented, young man with a golden horn, is not only a national jazz attraction, but the Quad-City Times Bix 7 run is a major American marathon, attracting 20,000 runners.

Always, it seems, the tier of Eastern Iowa cities and counties lean toward the Mississippi River. Dubuque, Iowa's oldest city, is an enchanting American portrait. The wealth came early with the lead trade. Passengers hang on tightly to ride the city's Fenelon Street Cable Car Railway to the mansioned bluffs.

McGregor is tantamount to autumn color, when the maples turn to chandeliers of golden leaves. In Iowa, autumn doesn't get better than this, and there are side trips from the paint-box country lanes to the 100,000 prehistoric Indian mounds, some in the prehistoric shape of bears and birds. Pull on a sweater and shiver through Spook Cave while you're there.

Downstream at Burlington, everyone *must* negotiate Snake Alley, a narrow brick street, 275 feet long, winding through five half-curves and two quarter-curves in a 58-foot descent. It was curved to ease the descent of horses and carriages, but its traffic today is even more popular than in the days of Dobbin. Whee! Like a carnival ride, but be sure your brakes are working. It's akin to San Francisco's storied Lombard Street.

In this wonderful Eastern Iowa land of the diamond-sparkling Mississippi River, industry and nodding tassels of corn, the crowning jewel is always the University of Iowa. Vance Bourjaily, one of the noted writers of our time, put it well:

"In those crop fields, beside the pasture, the corn is ankle-high and finger-flat, the fist-size soybean plants are Kelly green against black dirt. We had better wish them well. There's a tithe growing out there to keep the big University of Iowa moving on its earnest, complicated mission—for a cup of soybeans, your kids can triangulate a star; for an ear of corn, memorize two lines of Lermontov."

And Richard Rhodes, in his book *The Inland Ground,* summed it up:

"Iowa is more a demonstration farm than a place; more like some cosmic public relations project to prove that God's in his heaven and all's right with the world."

Amen!

Above: Time to harvest the oats, Amish style, near Kalona.
Right: Spend a day at Maquoketa Caves State Park, with its 13 limestone caves and a natural bridge that rises more than 40 feet.

Perhaps Aldo Leopold was looking upon a scene such as this Scott County summer when he said, "Conservation is a state of harmony between men and land."

Cedar Rapids came into being with broadsides of the 1840s making "particular reference to the convenience of the county and the healthfulness of the location." Some things never change.

Left: Like father…Ron Mullikin and son Shane, Washington County.
Below: Wool gathering on a mild Johnson County day.

KENNETH LAYMAN

Left: Take a ride to Fenelon Place on Dubuque's incline railway for a spectacular view of the Mississippi River and three of Iowa's neighbor states. Below: This almost-century-old gem is in Stone City, birthplace of Grant Wood.

Far left: Just another typical day in Bellevue along the Mississippi.

Right: The Mississippi River delivering up some fun—Harpers Ferry. Below: Allamakee County summer leaving in a blaze of glory.

Far right: A Mississippi River aerial, near Muscatine.

Above: Near Muscatine.
Right: What do you do in the winter if you live in Harpers Ferry?
Top: Burlington cityscape.

Left: The crowning jewel of Eastern Iowa, the University of Iowa.
Below: The essence of Quaker Oats in Cedar Rapids reminds visitors of breakfast time.

KENNETH LAYMAN

JANE REIMERS

Above: Washington County.
Right: Iowa City's Old Capitol.

24

A celebration of grand American traditions on the upper Mississippi.

Above: Near Waukon.
Right: Farm equipment auction near Kalona, sometimes known as Amish-land.

Facing page, top: Effigy Mounds National Monument.
Bottom left: Dyersville sports.
Bottom right: Elkader high school football.

The Iowa sun will not let a little morning fog stop it from brightening this farm near Volga.

Above: The Quad-Cities Centennial Bridge, landmark and path between neighbors.
Right: Reflections on the Mississippi.

Right: A little help from a friend.
Below: Soaking in Southern Iowa.

Facing page: From soybeans to scenery…

SOUTHERN IOWA

by Tricia DeWall

Margaret Slepsky owns and operates a travel agency in Atlantic. Every day, she sells plane tickets and plans trips to far-off places. Of the 80 countries she has ventured to, she thinks Iowa is the best place to be. She said it is where she belongs.

Marcella Howe of Creston began teaching school at age 17, when many of Iowa's teachers were fighting the second world war. Marcella retired in 1994—50 years and hundreds of students later—proud to have been part of one of the best education systems in America.

Fred Cobler lives only a few miles from the Wapello County farmhouse where he was born in 1927. He never has wanted to live anywhere else. He said he never will.

"Home is where you make it, but to me and my family, this is home," Cobler said. "I've been from coast to coast, and I know we live in the most blessed part of the whole world."

Southern Iowa is home to Margaret Slepsky, Marcella Howe and Fred Cobler. It also is home to thousands of others who enjoy the peacefulness of the countryside, the open land and the hardworking people who have made the state what it is today.

Many southeast Iowa counties were the first areas established when settlers began making their way westward across the barren land in the early 1880s.

The first Iowans made peace with the Native Americans who occupied the area—the Sauk and Fox tribes—and began clearing the land to make it suitable for tilling and growing crops. The settlers staked claims for homesteads and were proud to have land they could call their own. By the late 1880s, more settlers with ties to countries spanning the world—Germany, Czechoslovakia, the Netherlands and many other places—had arrived in Southern Iowa. They brought their own customs, traditions and religions, many of which are still alive today.

A large population of Old Order Amish, a Mennonite group with Swiss roots, lives near Bloomfield in Davis County. They often are referred to as "the buggy people" because they refuse to drive modern-day automobiles and rely on the horse and buggy for transportation. They believe God wants them to live as their people always have in the past. This means they do not live in towns, but on farms. They use workhorses to plow the fields and do not use commercial fertilizers, herbicides or insecticides—the way most Iowans farmed in the early 1900s.

Jersey calves in Southern Iowa.

People living in Bentonsport, a national historic district in Van Buren County, have also maintained traditional ways of living and live by the standards of good old-fashioned hard work. Bentonsport is one of Iowa's oldest towns, settled in the mid-1830s along the Des Moines River. Mormon artisans who dropped out of their trek across the country constructed brick and stone buildings and began paper mills and pottery houses. Centuries later, the buildings still are standing and residents still make old-world handicrafts every day of the week.

The railroad was a key factor in the development of Southern Iowa during the 1880s and 1890s, and remains an integral part of the area's continued development.

As hundreds of miles of track were laid, depots were built and towns sprang up around them. Many towns and cities of today, like Creston, Atlantic and Ottumwa, have the early train depots to thank for their beginnings more than 100 years ago. The railroads brought more settlers and simplified life for people who made their homes in the area. By the turn of the 20th century, railroads linked the state to the rest of the nation.

The development of the railroad also led to the development of industry in Southern Iowa. A variety of products derived from the area's rich earth—grain, coal, limestone and meat—now could be transported to other parts of the country.

Meatpacking was one industry made possible by the tracks, which hauled in livestock for slaughter and hauled away meat products. Over the years, the industry also enticed thousands of people to Southeast Iowa for good-paying jobs. John Morrell & Co., located in Ottumwa from 1888 to 1973, was once the world's largest pork processing plant. Thomas D. Foster, an early president of the England-born company, chose Ottumwa as the headquarters for the business for many of the same reasons people choose to make their home in Southern Iowa today.

"I chose Ottumwa because of the railroad facilities, the abundant water supply, the natural beauty of the city and the friendliness of the people," Foster is quoted as saying.

Other industries also have planted their roots in Southern Iowa and have become a driving force in the local economies of many towns and cities. Creston is the home of Bunn-o-matic, a coffeepot manufacturing plant, and the only North American site where Gummy Bears, a sweet and chewy candy, are made. Glacier Vandervell, a factory that manufactures parts for automobiles and rocketships, is Atlantic's largest employer. The town also has a Campbell's Chicken Soup factory. John Deere Ottumwa Works, a farm equipment manufacturer, and Excel, a pork processing plant, make their

home in Ottumwa. In nearby Eddyville is Cargill, a corn wet-milling plant. Rockwell International, a manufacturer of drive lines for heavy-duty trucks, is located in Fairfield. A 3M Scotch Tape plant and a Hormel meatpacking plant are the leaders in Knoxville's business district. Each of these industries has helped maintain thriving communities, providing thousands of jobs and a wealth of products sold locally and worldwide.

Coal mines also dotted Southern Iowa hillsides, some of which show the scars created by miners who stripped them of their treasure many years ago. The two large mining districts were Muchakinock in Mahaska County and Buxton in Monroe

A friend in need is a friend indeed.

County. Lucas and Keokuk counties also produced large quantities of the natural fuel. At first, coal was used only to heat homes and businesses, but as the railroads expanded, coal was in high demand to provide steam power to run the trains.

Buxton was the largest coal camp in the state, recording populations as high as 2,000 in the 1910 census. But, like most of the other mining camps, Buxton disappeared with the dwindling supply and demand for coal.

Agriculture, however, remains the most important industry in Southern Iowa. Farms produce thousands of acres of corn and soybeans. Cattle, hogs and sheep are also raised on the land. But the family farm isn't what it used to be.

There are fewer Southern Iowa farms in existence today, and the size of these farms is much larger. In 1923, there were 42,840 family farms in the 21 Southern Iowa counties. The average size of a farm was 152 acres. By 1993, the number of farms had dropped to 17,390, while the average size

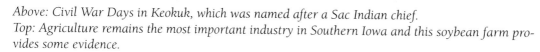

Above: Civil War Days in Keokuk, which was named after a Sac Indian chief.
Top: Agriculture remains the most important industry in Southern Iowa and this soybean farm provides some evidence.

early president of the England-born company, chose Ottumwa as the head-quarters for the business for many of the same reasons people choose to make their home in Southern Iowa today.

"I chose Ottumwa because of the railroad facilities, the abundant water supply, the natural beauty of the city and the friendliness of the people," Foster is quoted as saying.

Other industries also have planted their roots in Southern Iowa and have become a driving force in the local economies of many towns and cities. Creston is the home of Bunn-o-matic, a coffeepot manufacturing plant, and the only North American site where Gummy Bears, a sweet and chewy candy, are made. Glacier Vandervell, a factory that manufactures parts for automobiles and rocketships, is Atlantic's largest employer. The town also has a Campbell's Chicken Soup factory. John Deere Ottumwa Works, a farm equipment manufacturer, and Excel, a pork processing plant, make their home in Ottumwa. In nearby Eddyville is Cargill, a corn wet-milling plant. Rockwell International, a manufacturer of drive lines for heavy-duty trucks, is located in Fairfield. A 3M Scotch Tape plant and a Hormel meatpacking plant are the leaders in Knoxville's business district. Each of these industries has helped maintain thriving communities, providing thousands of jobs and a wealth of products sold locally and world-wide.

A friend in need is a friend indeed.

Coal mines also dotted Southern Iowa hillsides, some of which show the scars created by miners who stripped them of their treasure many years ago. The two large mining districts were Muchakinock in Mahaska County and Buxton in Monroe County. Lucas and Keokuk counties also produced large quantities of the natural fuel. At first, coal was used only to heat homes and businesses, but as the railroads expanded, coal was in high demand to provide steam power to run the trains.

Buxton was the largest coal camp in the state, recording populations as high as 2,000 in the 1910 census. But, like most of the other mining camps, Buxton disappeared with the dwindling supply and demand for coal.

Agriculture, however, remains the most important industry in Southern Iowa. Farms produce thousands of acres of corn and soybeans. Cattle, hogs and sheep are also raised on the land. But the family farm isn't what it used to be.

There are fewer Southern Iowa farms in existence today, and the size of these farms is much larger. In 1923, there were 42,840 family farms in the 21 Southern Iowa counties. The average size of a farm was 152 acres. By 1993, the number of farms had dropped to 17,390, while the average size

Right: Grant Wood's painting "American Gothic" made this Eldon house famous.
Below: The sun beams on Oskaloosa.

had grown to 376 acres. Farming in the 1990s has become an industry where only the large survive. Fred Cobler and his seven sons are among the survivors, he said, because farming is in their blood.

"We are becoming a minority and that concerns me," Cobler said. "But my sons and I feel it is a real privilege to be an American farmer. Sometimes it doesn't pay off financially, but there's so many other benefits that people sometimes forget about."

Iowa's southern tier is not only a land of corn and soybeans, it is a land of rolling hills, where a person can look to the horizon and see leafy treetops, a farmhouse or the grain elevator of a nearby town in the distance. Southern Iowa is a land of people who enjoy being absent from the hustle and bustle of city life, where these same people greet friends and strangers alike with a warmhearted hello. Southern Iowa also is a land of people who have not forgotten the simple pleasures in life, or the God who graced them with His goodness.

"The people are so nice here," Slepsky said of her hometown of Atlantic. "It's just a pleasant place to be."

Southern Iowans enjoy the natural beauty of the land they call home. From Pleasant Plain to New Market, and from What Cheer to Garden Grove, springtime brings the joyous songs of red-breasted robins returning from their winter homes. By the Fourth of July, temperatures are scorching, the air is humid and the corn is taller than knee-high. Autumn brings picturesque landscapes of yellow, auburn and red leaves, and draws people to places like The Cinder Path near Chariton, where some of the most beautiful fall colors can be seen. Southern Iowa winters are mild compared to other parts of the state. Temperatures aren't quite as bone-chilling and the snowfalls aren't quite as heavy.

Southern Iowa is home to some of the most scenic places in the state. Lake Rathbun in Appanoose County is Iowa's largest body of water and is a mecca for sunbathers and boaters in the summer and is a popular fishing hole year round. The white frame house with a thin, pointed upstairs window depicted in Grant Wood's painting "American Gothic" is located in Eldon. The painting made Grant Wood and the house famous in the early 1900s.

One of the area's most wonderful spots, made famous by college business-professor-turned-author Robert James Waller, is Madison County and its six covered bridges. After Waller wrote the best-selling romance novel, *The Bridges of Madison County,* Hollywood turned the poignant love story of Francesca Johnson and Robert Kincaid into a movie during the summer of 1994.

Christie Brittain of the Winterset Chamber of Commerce said the bridges were an "ordinary part of life" near the town of 4,000 until Waller's book hit the shelves in the spring of 1992. The most famous of the bridges is Cedar Bridge, which was built in 1883 by Benton Jones. It is the only bridge of the six that vehicles still are allowed to cross.

Adair's water-tower welcome.

The lively spirit of Southern Iowa has remained the same over the past 150 years, and it shows in the many activities and events that receive overwhelming support and attention. In towns large and small, people gather and cheer for their local high school football teams on chilly fall evenings. Southern Iowans are crazy about car racing. Knoxville is the home of national sprint car races and the national sprint car museum. National hot air balloon races are a late summer tradition in Indianola. Across the area, July and August bring county fairs—a time for youth to show off their handiwork or prize calf, and a time for carnival rides, cotton candy and funnel cakes.

The Southern Iowa spirit is alive today because people truly enjoy the state that they live in. Marcella Howe believes Iowa is the place where the grass is greener—and the air is fresher.

"I like the wide open spaces. I like that Iowa is quiet," she said. "We have good land and we raise crops. We have lots going here."

While no one knows what the next 150 years have in store, some things never will change. Southern Iowans will always be fun-loving people who believe old-fashioned hard work never goes out of style. For generations to come, families will gather around the dinner table to thank the Lord for the home-cooked meals before them. They never will take Iowa for granted, for it is the place they call home.

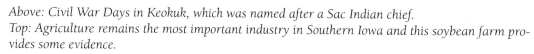

Above: Civil War Days in Keokuk, which was named after a Sac Indian chief.
Top: Agriculture remains the most important industry in Southern Iowa and this soybean farm provides some evidence.

The Roseman covered bridge. The six Madison County bridges were an ordinary part of life near Winterset until they were made famous by novelist Robert Waller.

A new day at the Imes/King covered bridge, which was built in 1870.

Left: A new season, time to plant.
Below: Autumn begins its arrival
to the corn and soybean fields
near Bloomfield.

Above: The annual Indianola hot-air balloon rally adds still more color to the countryside.

Facing page, top: Knoxville is home to the national sprint car races and sprint car museum.
Bottom: Southern Iowa means fun with friends.

JIM HAMANN/OTTUMWA COURIER

JIM HAMANN/OTTUMWA COURIER

MORNING STAR PHOTO

MORNING STAR PHOTO

Above: Who can resist another look at the Roseman Bridge, especially in the summer?

Left: And he gave it for his opinion, that whoever could make two ears of corn or two blades of grass to grow in a spot of ground where only one grew before, would deserve better of mankind, and do more essential service to his country, than the whole race of politicians put together. *Jonathan Swift*

Far left: Divided attention, in Blakesburg.

MORNING STAR PHOTO

Left: Chelsea Stanback and a Jersey calf share a Christmas hug in Fairfield.
Below: Places to go and things to see, Ottumwa.

Facing page, top: Fairfield field agobble with turkeys.
Bottom: Little League is big in Fairfield.

P. MICHAEL WHYE

Hidden potential.

Left: Realized potential.
Below: Thank you, thank you, thank you!

Above: Heritage stays alive with the help of a Mesquaki dancer at the powwow in Tama.
Right: A beautiful day to appreciate Pella's strong Dutch roots.

Facing page: An important capital city scene, the Des Moines River.

GREG RYAN & SALLY BEYER

CENTRAL IOWA

by Jeffrey Bruner

They came for the land.

Granted, that can be written about the origins of any Western or Midwestern state in America. But in Iowa, the dark rich soil reduces just about every other piece of ground in the United States to the status of mere dirt.

When white settlers came here, they saw what had attracted the Sauk and Meskwaki Indians many years earlier—a vast tallgrass prairie that covered most of Iowa as well as 12 other states in the Midwest. And settlers soon discovered that it was the prairie that helped create the rich soil that had made Iowa, agriculturally, the envy of the nation and a "breadbasket for the world."

Way back in 1856, Polk County—now home to more than 300,000 people—didn't have a lot of residents, but half of them farmed the land. Some grew spring and winter wheat, others planted oaks and potatoes and yet others grew corn. And they raised hogs and cattle.

Many Iowans today no longer farm the land. And those who do have specialized—wheat is now the domain of Kansas farmers while corn and soybeans dominate the Iowa farmland. But our heritage, even in the part of the state with its largest metropolitan area, still dates back to the land and how our ancestors found a way to make a life from it.

It's fitting that the land gave birth to the Iowa State Agricultural College and Model Farm, now known as Iowa State University. In 1862, the Morrill

Land Grant College Act offered land to states willing to start colleges to teach agricultural and mechanical arts.

State lawmakers, knowing a good deal when they saw one, agreed to the offer and got 203,000 acres of land in the process. Six years later, the college started.

For as long as the University of Iowa has been linked with liberal arts and professional programs like medicine and law, Iowa State has been linked with the land—a sort of "Moo U," to take the name of the fictitious land-grant university that is the subject of Iowa author Jane Smiley's 1995 best-selling novel.

It was research at Iowa State on hybrid seed corn in the 1920s that led to a revolution in agriculture in Iowa and the world, as well as the birth of one of the state's biggest companies.

JACK OLSON

It's tulip time in Pella.

The research intrigued Henry Wallace, who had been interested in genetics and plant breeding ever since he studied at Iowa State under George Washington Carver.

Wallace and a Coon Rapids farmer and salesman, Roswell Garst, formed the Pioneer Seed Corn Company to market hybrid corn to farmers, who were initially reluctant but were willing to try new things once the Great Depression enveloped the nation.

The events that really changed farmers were the droughts of 1934 and 1936, says Owen Newlin, a member of Pioneer's board of directors. "Hybrids did better than open pollinated varieties. And the hybrids yielded more and they stood up better. It was something that the farmers could see."

Fifteen years later, hybrid seed corn was planted on nearly every acre of corn in the state. Yields soared. And today, the Johnston-based Pioneer Hi-Bred International is a giant in agribusiness and the state's most valuable company. (Pioneer is responsible for half of Johnston's tax base and employs 1,000 people.)

Hybrid seed corn also gave birth to a new rite of passage for Iowa's children—detasseling corn. For the past 60 years, many teenagers and college students have held summer jobs walking down row after row.

"Hybrid corn probably did as much to bring the town youth to the country as consolidated schools and automobiles did to bring the country youth to the town," Iowa historian Joseph Wall once wrote.

And as for Garst, who parted ways with Wallace eventually, he went on to stake his claim in history. Garst sold 5,000 tons of hybrid seed corn to the Soviet Union and convinced Soviet leader Nikita Khrushchev to visit his farm in Coon Rapids in 1959 during the Cold War.

Even before Iowa became a state, Fort Des Moines and Iowa City—the site of the territorial capital—were fighting to be the site of the state capital.

Author George Sargent put his money on Iowa City.

In 1848, he wrote in his guidebook to Iowa, "No one appears to entertain a serious idea that the seat of government will be removed from [Iowa City], at least, for the next 50 years."

He was only off by 43 years.

After considerable political wrangling, the General Assembly decided in 1855 that the state capital would be moved to the center of the state in Polk County. The records of the state were later carried from Iowa City on ox-drawn bobsleds.

Tiny Fort Des Moines would never be the same.

The town eventually became just Des Moines. Its first council had seven wards—four west of the Des Moines River and three east. The rivalry between "east siders" and "west siders" has remained ever since.

The east siders won the battle for the capitol—and the state's fairgrounds, which draw hundreds of thousands of people annually for corn dogs, the midway, and the butter cow, a unique sculpture. More growth, however, has happened in the west side, where the construction of an interstate highway through the city allowed suburbs to thrive.

Almost from the start, insurance companies were a key part of the state. And, not surprisingly, their rise was also tied to the land.

And there's dancing in the streets when it's tulip time.

In 1867, young F.M. Hubbell and 15 of his friends formed the Equitable Life Insurance Company of Iowa. The idea was that company could raise money to invest in the state's agricultural economy if Iowans could be convinced to buy life insurance.

The idea worked—and soon an industry was booming. Soon Des Moines became known as the "Hartford of the Midwest." By 1888, eleven insurance companies made Des Moines their home and that number quadrupled in another 20 years.

Among those early insurance companies was Bankers Life, which 106 years later became The Principal, in 1985. The Principal has become Iowa's biggest insurance company, a multibillion-dollar firm that employs more than 6,000 people just in Des Moines.

Rapidly, Des Moines had become an insurance center and its insurance companies have shaped the city's skyline. Equitable's 18-story office building immediately became one of Des Moines' most distinctive buildings. More recently, the Principal Financial Group's 44-story skyscraper downtown added yet another peak to the skyline.

The land also led to the rise of one of the city's best-known companies, the Meredith Corporation.

Edwin T. Meredith, having inherited the weekly Populist publication *Farmers' Tribune* as a wedding gift in 1895, turned the publishing company around. He launched *Successful Farming*—which was devoted entirely to agriculture—in 1902.

Twenty years later, Meredith launched what is now one of the nation's best-known magazines, *Fruit Garden and Home*. Most of us know the magazine by its current name, *Better Homes and Gardens*.

Meredith served as agriculture secretary under President Woodrow Wilson and he was mentioned as a possible presidential candidate for the Democratic Party. Health problems, however, cut short his political ambitions.

Today, Meredith still publishes *Better Homes and Gardens* and *Successful Farming*—and a host of other publications from *Country America* to *Wood* to *home garden* and *Traditional Home*.

Iowa's flag and Capitol are reflected on the Vietnam Memorial at Des Moines.

The reasons Iowans settled here are many—some came for the land and the opportunity, some came as businessmen to fill the needs of settlers and yet others came here because they found freedoms here not available elsewhere.

Like any places settled by immigrants and pioneers, there are ethnic "enclaves" in this part of the state. Pella and the Amana Colonies are perhaps the best known—Pella's famous tulip festival in May draws Iowans from all over, while the colonies have become the state's top tourist attraction. (Amana also has evolved into a major industry, making anything from appliances to woolens to baked bread. And Pella, too, is now known nationwide for its Pella Windows.)

Iowans had different reasons for settling here but all came to make a better life. Three very different people would leave Central Iowa to affect the world in very different ways.

Long before modern-day people tarnished the meaning of the word "evangelist," there was Billy Sunday, an Ames preacher who gained more attention than many of the presidents of his day. (He also played professional baseball during the 1880s, setting the National League record for stolen bases that would later be broken by Ty Cobb.)

It was in the pulpit that Sunday became famous. He railed against the evils of sin and his colorful orations drew the masses in both the big cities and small towns—some towns built buildings just for his revivals.

"Some folks say a revival is only temporary," he once said. "So is a bath, but everybody needs one."

And it seems that nearly everybody heard Sunday at some time. It's been estimated that 80-100 million people heard his sermons, and without the benefit of television or radio.

At about the same time Sunday was growing up in Story County, a young

A look from the Capitol at downtown Des Moines provides a treat for the eye.

girl was being raised on a farm outside Charles City. Carrie Chapman Catt would help change politics forever for women in America.

When Catt became assistant editor of the *Mason City Republican* (her husband Leo was editor), she wrote a column called "Women's World." It didn't deal with food and fashion—but economic, social and legal issues.

In 1900, she became president of the National American Woman Suffrage Association. She gave speeches around the nation and around the world, talking about why women should have the right to vote.

Twenty years later, a constitutional amendment gave women the right to vote.

Iowa women didn't waste any time before taking advantage of their newly-won right. On August 27, 1920, one day after the Constitutional amendment was ratified, a Cedar Falls woman became the first woman in Iowa—and perhaps the nation—to vote.

Having helped win a 50-year battle, Catt was not content to rest. She spent the rest of her life fighting for the creation of the League of Nations and, later, the United Nations.

The organization that Catt helped start 75 years ago, the League of Women Voters, now has 1,000 state and local chapters.

And then there was George Washington Carver, who overcome obstacles to become one of the nation's most famous scientists. Born a slave in Missouri, Carver was educated at two Iowa universities—Simpson College in

53

Iowa State University in Ames offers resident and visitor alike an excellent atmosphere.

Indianola and Iowa State University in Ames—after he had been rejected by a Kansas college because he was African-American.

Carver became Iowa State's first African-American faculty member. At the age of 32 he was lured away by Booker T. Washington to become chairman of the Alabama university now known as the Tuskegee Institute.

To say that Carver was ahead of his time is an understatement. He changed Southern agriculture forever, pushing the concept of crop rotation and discovering more than 300 products that could be made from peanuts—from soap and ink to instant coffee. He also created new uses for sweet potatoes, cotton stalks, waste wood shavings as well as new foods, medicines, cosmetics, paper and silk.

Central Iowa—and the rest of the state—was not originally acre after acre of perfectly planted corn and soybeans.

The prairies were sacrificed for corn and soybeans and other indicators of progress like housing developments, freeways and parks. Almost all of the state's original prairie land was uprooted.

But today Iowans are giving back to the land. The prairie is coming back.

The Walnut Creek National Wildlife Refuge in Jasper County is 8,654 acres of restored prairie that is being rebuilt from the pockets of virgin prairie in the region.

And while most of Iowa will remain planted with soybeans and corns, in a small part of this land, parents and their children now can stand at sunset among the shooting star, the June grass and the blueflag iris and understand the almost limitless land and opportunities the pioneers saw here 150 years ago.

Several more reasons to call Central Iowa home.

Drake University provides more evidence that education is one of Iowa's primary values.

Top: An ag show in the Amana Colonies offers a colorful way of doing essential business.
Above: One of the treats on the Boone and Scenic Valley Railroad is crossing the 156-foot-high trestle on the 14-mile tour through the Des Moines River Valley.

Right: Pella Tulip Time, where romance is always in the air.
Below: Besides the usual wonders of such a place, the Des Moines Botanical Center adds the delight of free-flying birds.

Facing page: Seasonal garb in Waterloo.

The capital city.

Right: Terrace Hill, site of the Governor's Mansion.
Below: The 100-foot campanile at Iowa State University in Ames houses a 50-bell carillon.

Facing page: Yes, that is 22-karat gold leaf adorning the Capitol dome.

Above: Midsummer routine near Carroll.

Facing page, top left: Lest we forget the essential Iowa…
Top right: It's never difficult to keep an interested audience at the Living History Farm.
Bottom: What better place to have a July 4th air show than Independence?

Left: If you're near Des Moines, how about a Victorian holiday at the Living History Farms? Below: Shadows of a mill on the North Skunk River.

Facing page: Central Iowa can still show you a cattle drive, this one from Deep River, Poweshiek County.

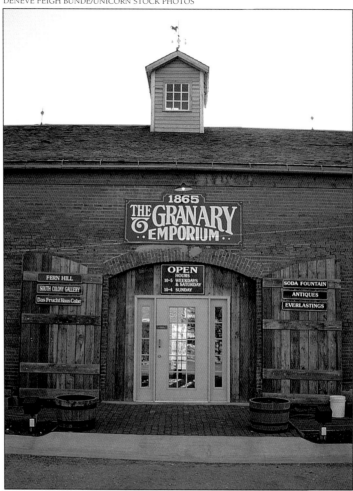

This page: The Amana Colonies lend an Old World comfortable feel.

Facing page: Under the Capitol dome.

LARSH K. BRISTOL

Right: The most important crops of North-ern Iowa.
Below: Is this what a "bean counter" does in Kossuth County?

Facing page: Another day to gladden the heart, near Burr Oak.

P. MICHAEL WHYE

NORTHERN IOWA

by Tom Thoma

How little we think of the dead. The land they cultivated, the houses they built, the work of their hands before us. We travel the same road, walk the same path, sit at the same fireside, sleep in the same room, ride in the same carriage and dine at the same table, yet seldom remember that those who once occupied those places are gone.
— The *Des Moines Star,* an Iowa newspaper of the 1850s

We are of the north. We are Iowans, to be sure. So much alike those from other corners and counties of the state. But in so many ways, so different. At least, we think we are.

Our climate is colder. The average temperature in the north is 18° in January, when the snow is knee-high, and 74° in July, when the corn is even higher. The southern section averages, by our standards, a balmy 24° in January and 77° in July.

We average 50 inches of snow; the south, a mere 22.

The differences may not seem that great, but still we fancy ourselves to be a heartier lot.

There is something about being from the north, too, that sometimes gives us a different sense of belonging. While other parts of the state are pulled toward Des Moines or Omaha or even Chicago, we feel an attraction to the shopping, the sporting events, the cultural opportunities of the Twin Cities of Minnesota.

It has been said, in fact, that the upper tier of Iowa counties are more like Minnesota than the rest of Iowa, both in geography and the people. But that's where any similarity ends.

Our rivalries are fierce. We believe there is nothing Minnesotans have that is better than what we have, that they can do nothing better than we can do.

Meredith Willson, the native son of Mason City who gave a Midwestern charge to the lights of Broadway, called it "Iowa Stubborn."

"...We're so by-God stubborn, we can stand touching noses for a week at a time and never see eye to eye..."

Willson, too, saluted our compassion for others with the very next line from that song in his famous play and movie, *The Music Man.*

STEPHEN GASSMAN

In Northern Iowa, this is what happens to the hay made while the sun shone.

"...We'll give you our shirt and the back to go with it if your crops should happen to die..."

Meredith Willson is one of our many famous native sons. But maybe no one touched as many millions as he did with his film and stage works, *The Music Man* and *The Unsinkable Molly Brown.* He even gave us something to cheer about with rousers for our state universities.

His music is just a small part of our history that stimulates the senses. Close your eyes, hum the tune and you can see them coming down the street...

"Seventy-six trombones led the big parade..."

Look to the East not so very far and hear the dramatic, stirring strains of the famed Bohemian composer, Antonin Dvorak, who left his native land for the National Conservatory of Music in New York City. Lonely for his native traditions, he found his way in 1893 to Spillville, the little Czech village in northeastern Iowa.

While there, he kept busy, worked on his *New World Symphony,* playing the St. Wenceslaus church organ and composing several chamber pieces. While his music has been described as elegant and noble, his inspirations came from a simple place: the banks of the Turkey River, where he formed ideas and jotted them on his shirt cuffs.

An Iowan, no. But he seemed infused with the Iowa spirit, a spirit tells us that there is no place like Iowa.

"That was an ideal spot," he said. "That's where I felt happy and I should have stayed there."

Loads of unloading goes on at Algona.

As stirring and lush as are Dvorak's melodies, there is another kind of beauty in Spillville, just as unique but truly Iowan.

It is the beauty of the hand-carved clocks of Frank and Joseph Bily. By trade, they were farmers and carpenters, but carving was always their hobby, one they engaged in diligently during the idle hours of long winters.

Most of their work was done in native wood, and they averaged one clock a year. One, their masterpiece, took from 1923 to 1927 to construct. Made of cherry and walnut, it stands 10 feet high. Its sides and front are covered with 57 scenes of American history. Its name, appropriately enough—"American Pioneer History Clock."

In 1949, their clocks were moved to the two-story building that was Dvorak's home and they carved two clocks in his honor.

From Spillville, it is not far over the gently rolling countryside to Nashua. The music lures you. Listen…

"Come, come, come, come…"

Come to the Little Brown Church in the Vale.

"…No spot is so dear to my childhood…"

The romance and beauty of the area just outside Nashua, called Bradford, so impressed a traveling man, Dr. William S. Pitts, that when he returned home to Wisconsin, he put his impressions to music.

The people of the area did indeed build a church. They painted it brown because it was the only color available.

Reid Erickson enjoys a bit of relaxation at an old one-room school near Decorah.

Pitts and his wife eventually moved to nearby Fredericksburg and he taught a singing class in Bradford. One night in 1864, he took the music with him and it was the beginning of one of the most endearing hymns ever.

Today, the Little Brown Church it is the site of hundreds of new beginnings as couples from around the country choose "The Little Brown Church in the Vale" to start their married lives together.

The rich musical history of North Iowa cannot be complete without a visit to the world-famous Surf Ballroom in Clear Lake.

Renovated in 1995, it is easy to stand on its wood floor and imagine the legendary sounds of the great big bands, like Duke Ellington and Benny Goodman. Almost anybody who was somebody played there.

And if you believe the music of Don McLean, then you believe "the music died" when a young Texan named Buddy Holly was killed in a plane crash just north of Clear Lake. The wreck also took the lives of The Big Bopper and Ritchie Valens, but it is Holly who is remembered most—and certainly most fondly.

His last performance was at the Surf. His music will last forever. "Peggy Sue," "That'll Be The Day," "Words of Love." It was music that so touched four young men from England that they took inspiration from Holly's band, The Crickets, to name their own group The Beatles.

McLean, in his musical tale, "American Pie," sang what many rock 'n' roll fans felt about Buddy Holly.

"...I can't remember if I cried when I heard about his widowed bride, but something touched me deep inside, the day the music died."

If the music of Broadway and rock 'n' roll is a significant part of our heritage, so is the music of the churches and its people, those who sought safety and security in new surroundings.

The Decorah area is famous for its Norwegian heritage, with Luther College and the Vesterheim Museum as its centerpieces.

Scandinavians made their way to Clayton County in 1848; others followed and settled in Fayette, Allamakee and Winnebago Counties.

The Irish located in Emmetsburg in Palo Alto County in 1859.

Some areas, such as Mason City, drew people of many backgrounds.

Art Fischbeck, a Mason City businessman who has devoted thousands of hours to preserving the region's history, said each group found its niche.

"The Greeks worked in the cement plants, the southern Europeans worked in the brickyards, the English worked in the meatpacking plant and the Mexicans worked in the sugar factories."

They coexisted, but it wasn't always peaceful. Stories of "Powder Street" clashes between the cultures are legendary. But they did coexist, finding prosperity (for the most part) and shelter.

Along with the beautiful churches that enhance our cities and countryside, an awe-inspiring monument to the region's strong religious background is the Grotto in West Bend. A sparkling monument, a feast for the eyes, it is a tribute to unwavering faith.

Life on the Hayden Prairie.

Father Paul Matthias Dobberstein, of German birth, was ordained into the priesthood in Milwaukee in 1897. Falling critically ill with pneumonia, he prayed and vowed that if he survived, he would build a shrine.

After ordination, he went to West Bend as a pastor and for more than a decade he collected rocks and semiprecious stones for his grotto. He started work in 1912; he finished in 1954. The grotto tells the story of the Redemption in the largest known shrine of its kind in the world.

The largest. The only. The last. The best. The biggest. The greatest. Such words are used often to describe North Iowa's accomplishments, its people, its attractions.

Fort Atkinson, in Winnishiek County, was built in 1840 and has the distinction of being the only fort ever built by the U.S. government to protect one Indian tribe—the peaceful Winnebagos—from their enemies, the Sioux and Sacs.

The first consolidated school west of the Mississippi was established in Buffalo Center in 1896. The communities of Buffalo Center, Rake, Lakota, Titonka and Thompson are part of that system today.

The Indian chiefs were described as no less than great. They included: "Mahaska," who was murdered by one of his own tribe after he caused some of his men to be arrested when government officials complained Indians were violating the laws; "Winneshiek," who claimed to see the dance of the departed in the Northern Lights, was loyal to and loved by his people; "Waukon-Decorah," chief of the Winnebagos who had their village near Decorah, was friendly to the white settlers and helped keep peace between the Indians and whites.

STEPHEN GASSMAN

Seeds that won't fall by the wayside.

In 1900, the Hart-Parr gas engine company—formed in Madison, Wisconsin, by a couple of Charlies, Hart and Parr—moved to Charles City in Floyd County. In the winter of 1900–01, the first gas traction engine, the forerunner of the modern tractor, was produced. Seven years later, the story goes, sales manager W.H. Williams was trying to think of a shorter word to describe the meaning of "gasoline traction engine." That word was "tractor."

Tractors are no longer made in Charles City, but a museum there sustains the story of these forerunners of today's giant farm machines that help feed the world by churning through our dark, rich soil.

The soil, rich and productive. The air, clean and invigorating. The waters, plentiful and so accessible to irrigate our crops, quench our thirst and give us outlets for recreation.

The glistening waters of Clear Lake, Storm Lake and the Great Lakes invite us to relax, to try our luck with a rod and reel, to do nothing more than sit at their shores and soak in their beauty that is refreshed each year by the spring thaws.

Clear Lake, in Cerro Gordo County, was formed by glaciers and was so large at one time that it was described as an inland sea.

Storm Lake, in Buena Vista County, got its name from the storms that form suddenly and whip up waves as they move along.

And Iowa has its own Great Lakes region, in Northwest Iowa.

There is Spirit Lake, where legend says Indians believed the Great Spirit ruled the waters, making them rough, smiling or sad.

East and West Okoboji lakes have been described as charming and beautiful. West Okoboji is one of three "blue lakes" in the world; the others are in Canada and Switzerland.

These Great Lakes have been an attraction since their discovery.

But there is a tragic chapter in the lakes' great history, the Spirit Lake

Spirit Lake of a summer's eve.

Massacre on March 8, 1857. Inkpaduta (Scarlet Point) led a band of Sioux that killed 32 settlers on the south shore of West Okoboji. Scarlet Point and his men escaped, and apparently were never punished.

But a monument makes sure we will never forget that tragedy.

It is one of many monuments all through this land of northern Iowa. Monuments to triumph and tragedy, to success and failure; monuments to our strong religious faith; monuments to the people who set the path for us and future generations.

"We travel the same road, walk the same path, sit at the same fireside, sleep in the same room, ride in the same carriage and dine at the same table…"

Off-season near Sioux Rapids.

Above: Deer were the first to hear the crunch of snow along Plum Creek.
Left: Winter sports on Smith Lake.

Left: And welcome to the fresh air of Northern Iowa.
Below: Fall falls.

Facing page: A find on the Upper Iowa River, Dunnings Spring.

Spillville's Bily Clocks are displayed in the former Dvorak residence. The American Pioneer History Clock stands near-ly ten feet high and has 52 panels.

MEREDITH WILLSON HOME
RENOVATION
Volunteers, Please Call 423-2765 or 424-9425

Above: "…We'll give you our shirt and the back to go with it if your crops should happen to die…"
Right: Boulder Park in Nora Springs.

Nashua's Church in the Wildwood, the Little Brown Church in the Vale, sees over 800 weddings a year.

JAMES BLANK

DENEVE FEIGH BUNDE/UNICORN STOCK PHOTOS

Above: RAGBRAI at the Grotto of the Redemption in West Bend.
Left: Luther College offers some fun and games.

Signs of the time, near Bristow.

Above: The Upper Iowa River and friends.
Right: Bullheads.

LARSH K. BRISTOL

GREG RYAN & SALLY BEYER

LARSH K. BRISTOL

88

Above: Twilight near Algona.

Facing page, top left: Indulging in Decorah's annual three-day Nordic Fest.
Right: Holiday cheer at Decorah's Vesterheim Norwegian-American Museum.
Bottom: A trip to the Old World looms at the Vesterheim.

Above: Good night, Lake Okoboji.

Facing page, top: To some, the Surf Ballroom in Clear Lake is where the music died; for others, it's one of the few places left to enjoy dancing to big-band and polka music.
Bottom: Play at work in Algona.

WESTERN IOWA

by Bill Zahren

When one famous Western Iowan lay propped against his horse on a Loess Hills bluff in 1845, he gazed upon the very strengths that still endure in Iowa 150 years later.

With the constant breezes that formed the bluff more than 12,000 years ago rippling through his horse's mane, Sioux Indian Chief War Eagle breathed the clean air and admired two great assets of Western Iowa—land and river.

When War Eagle died in 1851, his tribe buried him on that favorite bluff. In 1975, Indians and non-Indians marked his burial ground with a 31-foot stone and iron sculpture of War Eagle extending a peace pipe toward the Missouri and Big Sioux rivers below.

From War Eagle's bluff, now a city park, you can still see three of the elements that made Western Iowa and its residents what they are today.

Churning through the background is the Missouri River, the main channel of a centuries-old drainage system for the fertile land. The river joins with the Big Sioux River near War Eagle, marking the point where Iowa, South Dakota and Nebraska converge.

Down in the flats to War Eagle's left, the Missouri passes by modern downtown Sioux City briefly merging historic and modern Iowa.

This brief splash of urban Iowa is quickly drowned out by the endless patchworks of Iowa farm fields. The corn and soybeans sprout from some of the richest soil in the world cultivated by the most efficient food producers in history. Huge sections of the Missouri today remain lined with cottonwoods and cornfield as they have for a century.

Finally, from Loess Hills bluffs like War Eagle's, you can usually pick out two lines of steel bordered in green—railroad tracks—stretching like giant incisions through the agricultural patchwork.

Western Iowa grew up as a fusion of these sights—land, river, railroad. Each is connected to the other and plays a role in the Western Iowa mentality.

JAMES BLANK

Above: Clarinda, America.

Page 92: The Immemann Danish Lutheran Church in Monona County. P. MICHAEL WHYE PHOTO
Page 93: The Southwood Preserve in Woodbury County.

The main attraction in the west is still the land, its value magnified by the lack of cities covering it. Indians like War Eagle called the land "Mother Earth" and revered it as the supplier of their food, clothing and shelter. Modern farmers use an ever more sophisticated series of tools to work the land but still share much the same affection for it as Indians and early white settlers.

Each morning in Western Iowa, rush-hour noises consist of gravel crunching under your boots, the rhythmic flopping of opening and closing hog-feeder lids, the beller of cattle and rustling of a few million corn and soybean plants.

The noon rush in most any Western Iowa small town features streets lined with pickups and local cafes full of farmers. The noon meal at the cafe—we eat "dinner" at noon and "supper" at night—is a chance for farmers to meet and talk about common concerns and joys—weather, markets, politics, children.

The link to the land even affects the pace of life in rural Iowa. Crops and livestock only grow so fast and raising either teaches patience. Everything waits for the weather.

Catherine White, a Harlan native who now lives in Omaha and is executive director of the historic Dodge House in Council Bluffs, has found that this version of Iowa travels very well indeed.

During vacation in Ireland a few years ago, White and her husband at first identified themselves as being from Omaha, thinking the urban center would be more widely known. When the Irish failed to recognize Omaha, the Whites tried identifying themselves as Iowans.

"They knew about Iowa," White says with a chuckle. "The image was farming—the bread basket of the country—and our high educational standards and teachers."

Even as farmer numbers dwindled over the decades, Iowa has held onto its rural feel. Western Iowa's two urban areas are filled with people who were born somewhere else. If not from the farm, then many of us come from small towns around the state.

Something about living so close to the land makes helping neighbors

The Council Bluffs home of Grenville M. Dodge, general and railroad builder, was built in 1869.

something of an instinct. "We still have those small town values," says Blair Chicoine, a river and railroad historian who runs a welcome center along Interstate 29 just downstream from War Eagle. "Historically you have very strong guidelines for hard work and cooperation. Neighbors had to help each other. The good times and the bad times, everyone shares them together."

It's a mix of honor, independence, Iowa stubbornness and genuine concern. It's the reason Iowans still smile and say "hello" to total strangers they pass in the streets, a ritual that can be quite disconcerting to visitors from larger urban areas.

The land and those small town values have attracted people to Iowa for all of its 150 years. The most recent immigrants have come to do the work needed to get Iowa cattle and hogs to America's grocery stores and restaurants.

That's the work of meatpacking plants, which have attracted successive waves of ethnic groups to Western Iowa. The main skill required for boning carcasses in a packing plant is the ability to use a knife. Speaking English is still largely optional. The job qualifications immediately attracted immigrants, first from western and central Europe. Later waves included Hispanic and Southeast Asian immigrants. Some members of each culture established residency in Iowa, gradually adding dimensions to the state's culture and hues to the collective urban skin color.

Today, a lot of little packing plants around Western Iowa have been replaced by a few large plants, but the immigrants still come.

War Eagle's people are still here too. Sioux City has a large population of urban Indians, and its proximity to reservations for the Winnebago, Omaha and Santee Sioux tribes in Nebraska injects a good bit of Indian culture into the city.

Lately, Indian and whites have both hit on the same economic development idea in Western Iowa—gambling—which has brought the riverboat back to the Missouri River.

The floating casino and restaurant, *Belle of Sioux City*, now cruises the Missouri River at Sioux City. Plans call for two more riverboats to enter the Missouri at Council Bluffs. Indian tribal lands near Onawa and Sloan now hold vast casinos that have generated millions for the Omaha and Winnebago people.

Riverboats are nothing new in Western Iowa, of course. They were the dominant mode of travel for about 70 years after Lewis and Clark first came up river in 1804. The commerce provided by their cargoes founded and sustained towns. "Wood hawks"—people who sold wood to power the boats—eventually became some of the first farmers and continued to rely on riverboats as the consumers of their produce and livestock.

While Sioux City's roots are firmly in the river, Council Bluffs' history is bound by railroads and wagon trains.

P. MICHAEL WHYE

The famous RAGBRAI race in Fremont, near Sidney.

Perhaps Council Bluff's most famous citizen, Maj. Gen. Grenville Dodge, first set eyes on what Lewis and Clark had called "council bluff" when he surveyed the area for a railroad line in 1853. Dodge was so fetched with the place that he decided to make it his home.

The bluffs in Council Bluffs are Loess (*luss*) Hills, created by drifting sediment after the glaciers withdrew thousands of years ago. An increasingly popular tourism attraction today, the Loess Hills are up to 200 feet tall and stretch for 200 miles, forming a hilly spine for Western Iowa and connecting Sioux City and Council Bluffs.

In early spring, the hills look like the enormous hunched backs of a large herd of grazing buffalo. In fall, foliage shrouds the hills in brilliant shades providing a stark contrast with the brown, ripening crops of the valleys and plains.

By the time Dodge came to Council Bluffs, it had been settled by Mormons who stopped there during their migration from Nauvoo, Illinois, to Salt Lake City. They called the town "Kanesville."

Before he was president, Abraham Lincoln met with Dodge in Council Bluffs to consider the emerging city as the launching point for the first transcontinental railroad. Dodge continued to lobby for his hometown, sending letters to railroad officials even while fighting in the Civil War.

Council Bluffs did eventually become the eastern terminus for the Transcontinental Railroad and Dodge went on to great wealth and fame as a railroad builder in the West. Omaha later proclaimed itself the eastern terminus and the people of Council Bluffs took the matter to the Supreme Court where they successfully defended the title.

From Council Bluffs, the railroad branched north and south, eventually connecting Sioux City and the rest of Western Iowa.

The rise of the railroad may have changed the way people got here, but the reason for coming remained the same.

"The river and the railroads were the methods," says Sioux City Public Museum Director Scott Sorensen. "The lure was the land."

Railroad land agents, not always of great moral character, fanned across the eastern United States and into Europe offering both real and imagined land tracts to immigrants. Groups of men from places like Holland, Germany, and Norway took the offer, came to Iowa and established farms. As soon as they had enough money, the pioneers would send for other friends and family members to join them. The settlement pattern created pockets of ethnicity around Western Iowa. Many places still celebrate their ethnic roots with annual festivals.

Railroads succeeded rivers as the lifeline for Western Iowa and the region began to fill in with towns. Railroad companies often simply started towns where they needed them, leaving Western Iowa with towns named after long-dead railroad executives.

P. MICHAEL WHYE

Looks like a Sidney Rodeo cowboy is about to launched.

Attracting a railroad to Western Iowa towns became the state's first form of economic development. Just as towns offer financial incentives to attract new business today, Iowa towns pursued railroads with great vigor in the late 19th century.

Railroads were a commercial lifeline, carrying farm produce to markets and bringing back consumer goods of all types. The first trains into a town were greeted like returning war heroes. When the first train arrived in Sioux City in 1868, the local paper's headline blared "SAVED AT LAST."

Economic development today has switched from attracting transportation to luring industry. Council Bluffs and Sioux City both pursue industry as vigorously as their ancestors pursued railroad connections.

Both cities have started paying less attention to state lines and more attention to cooperating with economic development efforts in Nebraska and South Dakota.

The old battle symbolized by Council Bluffs and Omaha both claiming to be the eastern terminus of the Transcontinental Railroad is "starting to become water under the bridge," says Kari Sliva, executive director of the Council Bluff's Convention and Visitors Bureau. Sioux City often presents a united front with South Sioux City, Nebraska, and North Sioux City, South Dakota, when chasing jobs.

In fact, much of Sioux City's recent economic development has happened

Why Iowa? Try a sunset in Lewis and Clark State Park on the Missouri River.

across the river in thriving business parks in North Sioux City.

Sliva says people in both towns are also starting to rediscover their river, trail and railroad heritage. She says a "tourism corridor" along both sides of the Missouri is forming as more people become interested in historic facts about the region.

Council Bluff's new riverboats plan huge developments on the city's riverfront. A multimillion-dollar National Western Historic Trails Center is also planned for the Council Bluff's riverfront. The center will focus on the California, the Lewis and Clark, and the Mormon trails, which all intersected in Council Bluffs.

Sioux City moved back to the river a bit before Council Bluffs when city government committed millions to redevelop a riverfront park downtown. The triangle of land that forms the very southeast tip of South Dakota—within view of War Eagle's grave—has been transformed into a plush golf course, business park and residential housing area.

While Western Iowa works to diversify its economy, there seems little danger that the heritage and economic power of agriculture will leave our end of the state anytime during the next 150 years. The view from War Eagle's Loess Hill perch still sends a shiver of appreciation through Western Iowans. It's like looking down at the past and future all at once—and being thankful for both.

Left: The Dodge House at Council Bluffs lets a Christmas imagination run wild.
Below: Front porches and the crunch of autumn leaves—such is life in Western Iowa.

Above: "Crops and livestock only grow so fast and raising either teaches patience," but there is satisfying result, one shown here at the Lyon County Fair in Rock Rapids.
Right: Yes, it's a real motel—one of the last of the old-timers—in Council Bluffs.

Facing page: Nature is well-preserved at the Fowler Nature Preserve in Woodbury County.

Above: Western Iowa's glorious Loess Hills, Southwood Nature Preserve. Right: Someone's watching the RAGBRAI enthusiasts as they cruise through Hawarden.

Facing page: Joe Pye (Eupatorium purpureum) *doing its share to color Snyder Bend Park.*

102

Perhaps a manned keelboat is an unusual sight elsewhere, but not in Lewis and Clark State Park, northwest of Onawa.

Left: The prairie coneflower (Ratibida tagetes) decorates Woodbury County near the Missouri. Below: There's always a lot going on in Council Bluffs, but the solitude of the Missouri remains an option.

Right: Upon a winter's day at Mount Crescent.
Below: A reminder in Council Bluffs of "the how" of Western Iowa's settlement.

Facing page, top: To all things there is a season in Rock Rapids.
Bottom: Western Iowans delight in the migration of geese at the DeSoto Bend National Wildlife Refuge.

As far as the eye can see, Murray Hill near the Little Sioux River gives an appreciation for the land and the air that is Western Iowa.

Left: A Western Iowa July 4th.
Below: The Tulip Festival Parade in Orange City.

Above: In 1975, Indians and non-Indians marked Chief War Eagle's burial ground with a 31-foot stone and iron sculpture of him extending a peace pipe toward the Missouri and Big Sioux rivers below. Top: Fowler Park in Woodbury County.

Ah, those Missouri River tugboats.

QUAD-CITY TIMES

Bill Wundram, Davenport, a *Quad-City Times* columnist, has been writing, he says, "since the lava dried." He is believed to be the only American columnist who writes a local column seven days a week.

"I've been doing it for a dozen years now. All it takes is a certain lack of imagination and an interest in not doing much of anything else," he says. "Really, I'm not a writer. I'm more of a storyteller. I just plow the fields daily, trying to pick up a few laughs and warm-fuzzies here and there to keep us from crying out."

M. SCOTT MAHASKEY

Tricia DeWall, 23, is among the third generation of her family to be born and raised in Iowa. She graduated from the University of Iowa in 1994 with a degree in journalism and currently works as a reporter at *The Ottumwa Courier.* A transplanted city girl, Tricia enjoys returning to her roots—a 500-acre farm near Pocahontas—to help her parents watch the corn and soybeans grow.

STEPHANIE BRUNER

Jeffrey Bruner covers higher education for *The Daily Tribune* in Ames. A native of Pittsburgh, Pennsylvania, he is a graduate of Drake University in Des Moines. He is married to Stephanie Polsley Bruner, who grew up on a farm in Page County. Iowa's special spirit and wonderful people continue to fascinate him.

MASON CITY GLOBE-GAZETTE

Tom Thoma, formerly the city editor, is now the sports editor of the *Globe-Gazette.* A native of Nora Springs, Thoma moved to Mason City as a tot, graduated from Mason City High, North Iowa Area Community College in Mason City, and Drake University in Des Moines. He has a radio show three mornings a week and is an avid—but terrible—golfer. He says, "It is with great appreciation and admiration that I acknowledge the use of two books for background: *Sixty Sketches of Iowa's Past and Present,* by William J. Wagner, and *Iowa The Beautiful Land: A History of Iowa,* by Jessie Merrill Dwelle. They helped refresh my memory and taught me many new things."

RHONDA ZAHREN

Bill Zahren is a fifth-generation Iowan born in Lake Park. He graduated from Harris-Lake Park High School in 1982 and earned a Bachelor of Arts degree in mass communications from Morningside College in 1986. He worked for two years at the Le Mars *Daily Sentinel* and has been with the *Sioux City Journal* since 1988. He lives with his wife, Rhonda, and their daughters, Haley and Jena, in Sioux City.